# COOKING

OY SCOUTS OF AMERICA
RVING, TEXAS

**1985 Printing of the
1967 Edition**

# REQUIREMENTS

1. Plan menus for 3 straight days (nine meals) of camping. Include the following:

(a) A camp dinner with soup; meat, fish, or chicken; two fresh vegetables; drink; and dessert. All are to be cooked.

(b) A one-pot dinner. Use foods other than canned.

(c) A breakfast, lunch, and dinner good for a trail or backpacking trip where light weight is important. Use as much dehydrated or dry frozen foods as you can. Get them from local food stores (not specialty stores). You should be able to store all foods used for several days without refrigeration. The lunch planned should not need cooking at the time of serving. The dinner must include hot soup or a salad; meat, fish, or chicken; vegetable and starch food or a second vegetable; baked biscuits; and drink. (The menus for the other two breakfasts and two lunches shall be the kind you can prepare in camp or on the trail.)

2. Do the following:

(a) Make a food list, showing cost and amount needed to feed three or more boys using the menus planned in requirement 1.

(b) List the utensils needed to cook and serve these meals.

(c) Figure the weight of the foods in requirement 1c.

3. Using the menus planned in requirement 1:

(a) Prepare and serve for yourself and two others the three dinners, the lunch, and the breakfast planned in requirement 1. Time your cooking so that each course will be ready to serve at the proper time.*

(b) For the meals prepared in requirement 3a, for which a fire is needed, pick a good spot for your fire. Build a fireplace. Include a support for your cooking utensils from rocks, logs, or like material. (Where local laws do not allow you to do this, the counselor may change it to meet the law.) The same fireplace may be used for more than one meal. Use charcoal as fuel in cooking at least one meal.

(c) For each meal prepared in requirement 3a, use safe food-handling practices. Use the correct way to get rid of garbage, cans, foil, paper, and other rubbish by burning and using a tote-litter bag. After each meal, clean up the site thoroughly.

Copyright 1967
Boy Scouts of America
Irving, Texas
ISBN 0-8395-3257-1
No. 3257    Printed in U.S.A.    20M385

---

*The meals in requirement 3a may be prepared for different trips. They need not be prepared consecutively. Scouts earning this badge in summer camp should plan around food they can get at the camp commissary.

# Contents

# PREPARE FOR AN ADVENTURE IN COOKING!

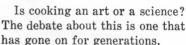

Is cooking an art or a science? The debate about this is one that has gone on for generations.

At the same time, the "ceremony" of eating has become a basic part of man's existence, whether food intake is crude and irregular as it might be in an aboriginal tribe or is an elegant and extended state banquet. The meals that you'll prepare in meeting the Cooking merit badge requirements, we hope, won't make you a member of one group or the other.

Gourmet or gourmand? Will you live to eat or eat to live? You may do some of both during your lifetime. From the experience and fun you'll have in cooking for yourself and your fellow Scouts, we can forecast an interest in food and its preparation that will last you all your life!

Another sure bet: Cooking for others will show you things about your fellow humans as clearly as any of life's experiences. While serving tasty meals to a hungry gang, you'll see a pattern beginning with nagging impatience, moving to a more peaceful time, and finally the pleasant after-effect of cheerful, quiet, and contented companionship.

So discover happy cooking outdoors. It's fun.

# A Balanced Diet

Planning a menu is a first-rate exercise in common sense.

"Minimum daily requirements" is a phrase that continues to be important to the cook, for the essentials of man's diet are measured by vitamins, minerals, fats, carbohydrates, and proteins.

You won't painstakingly count each of these for every meal that you'll consume on the trail, but your menus should include a decent balance of foods from the four basic groups.

These groups include: (a) meat, poultry, fish, eggs; (b) milk and milk products; (c) vegetables and fruits; (d) bread and other flour products. Fats, sweets, and flavorings are among the many "accessory" foods discussed, along with the foods from the other basic groups, later in this pamphlet.

The menus here will not follow the dieting approach—not at all. That is, we won't count out every calorie or nutrient of the foods for each menu.

At the same time, the experienced cook (indoor or outdoor style) often works more or less by intuition to furnish his hungry crew with the sort of balance that dietitians agree is best.

Until you develop that intuition (imagination is another term for it), it is best to stick to well-planned menus and familiar recipes.

## Variety, Nutrition, Convenience

When you and the gang have been hiking, exploring, boosting backpacks over the trail to camp, there's no argument about whether you eat to live or live to eat! The main point then is to fill plate and stomachs with all possible speed!

Naturally, this kind of efficiency calls for preplanning on your part — and a high order of planning, at that. "Convenience" on the trail, then, is one of three main goals in your menu planning. The balance of nutrition in these foods is already pretty well worked out for you, until you gain that needed intuition through cooking experience.

Plastic boxes,
tubes, bottles, fla[...]
and bags for
packing foods f[...]
breakable, overs[...]
heavy, or incon[...]
ient original cont[...]
ers. Check sec[...]
of caps; insert
to make tight s[...]
Tape loose lids.

# Packing Your Fo[...]

Take all you need for each meal in its most convenient form—light, flexible for easy packing; premeasured, premixed for no-waste, no-sweat preparation. It is essential that dehydrated foods be packaged in waterproof containers.

Food purchased in large quantities—or even in minimum quantities—should be repackaged for convenient toting and divided into one-meal portions. Good planning calls for it; your ability to prepare a good meal quickly "out there" over the fire demands it.

Pack foods so that each package holds enough for one meal. Breakfast and supper packages should hold enough ingredients for their share of the meals.

Cardboard containers usually don't pack conveniently, and are easily broken or crushed. The best repackaging plan calls for plastic refrigerator bags that you can seal with rubber bands or plastic-coated wire ties.

Guessing games are great fun in your entertainment program, but they have no place when you're hungry and want to identify the contents of a food package in a hurry. Tuck labels from the original packages into transparent storage bags so that they show plainly. Another real help is to have a recipe or two along with the product label in the plastic bag. This is an easy thing to do in most cases, because side panels of the ready-mix flours have recipes printed on them. Or, you can clip the recipes from this pamphlet and enclose them in a little dustproof individual plastic bag.

The last word in planning and preparation, is to mark packages to indicate quantity, content, the day, and the meal—along with instructions for preparation.

You should figure each man will carry an average of 2 pounds of food (dry weight) for each day's rations. This fact alone is a strong argument for the best possible planning. And that includes menus and the way that you'll stack and pack your food.

There's a fact that is ignored by most cookbooks designed for the kitchen: The amount of sweets and fats that you'll require in outdoor living is nearly double what you would ordinarily need. Know this and plan for it. It's sometimes a long hike back to the place where you can get high-calorie butter, lard, oleo-margarine, or cooking oils. The same thing is true for sugar in any form.

Your enthusiasm might make you want to just throw some things into your pack and roar off into the wilds. Aside from being potentially disastrous, such a gleeful approach can later completely take away the edge of pleasure that should be a basic reward of the well-prepared cook.

## Use a Checklist

Make a checklist with separate columns for each group of essentials. One column will be for dry foods, a second for perishables, another for canned goods, and still another for eating and cooking utensils.

It's wise to carry the check-off process to the point where you're absolutely sure that you have every ingredient for each of the recipes that you will use while faraway from your source of supplies. Another wise move is to be sure before you start just how many pots and other utensils you'll need for each of the planned meals.

Actual grouping of your food is worthwhile, too. That is, sort and classify both foods and utensils by stacking them on a large table on the porch or in the back-yard before you pack.

With either method—or working them together—you'll be able to check supplies against menus to be sure that no essential item is still on the kitchen table when you want it over your fire.

It's also a good idea to keep a record of everything you carry for future reference—including what's leftover at the end of your camping jaunt.

Menus

The next six pages contain menus that may give you ideas for the ones you are to plan for Requirement 1. Study them for balanced diet, and then substitute foods you like.

A sample breakfast, lunch, and dinner is shown. A food list has been developed for each menu. This is the kind you will make up for Requirement 2 and will give you ideas about quantities needed for six persons.

On page 93 the menu for "Slum Gullion" is broken down, showing a food list and the recipe.

For simple meals, make your lists directly from your menus. For more elaborate ones, you'll have to consult a cookbook for recipes before making your list. For example, you couldn't tell from the salmon dinner menu below that cornflakes, eggs, and onions were needed to make it, until you looked up a recipe for making salmon cakes.

## BREAKFAST

Sliced oranges
French toast
Bread and butter
Cereal
Syrup or jam
Cocoa
Milk

### FOOD LIST:

6 medium-size oranges
dry cereal, 6 servings
3 eggs
1 tall can evaporated milk
16 slices bread
3 tbsp. shortening

¼ lb. butter
1 1-pt. bottle syrup
1 8-oz. jar jam
¼ lb. ready-to-use cocoa
2 qts. milk
sugar

## LUNCH

Canned meat and lettuce sandwiches
Peanut butter and jelly sandwiches
Applesauce
Milk

### FOOD LIST:

2 8-oz. cans of pressed meat (such as Spam, Treet, Prem)
1 head lettuce
1 8-oz. jar peanut butter
1 8-oz. glass jelly

18 slices bread
¼ lb. butter
2 qts. milk
2 No. 2 cans applesauce
salt, pepper, mustard

## DINNER

Salmon cakes
Boiled potatoes
Buttered beans
Bread and butter
Cake with fruit sauce
Milk
Fruit drink

### FOOD LIST:

1 No. 2 can salmon
1/3 8-oz. box cornflakes
1 egg
1 medium-size onion
2 tbsp. shortening
2 No. 2 cans string beans
12 medium-size potatoes

12 slices bread
¼ lb. butter
2 qts. milk
2 pkgs. fruit drink powder
1 lb. poundcake
1 12-oz. jar preserves
salt, pepper, sugar

| 7-DAY SAMPLE MENU | | | | | | | | |
|---|---|---|---|---|---|---|---|---|
| Item | Source | Sun BLD | Mon BLD | Tue BLD | Wed BLD | Thu BLD | Fri BLD | Sat BLD |
| Dry cereal | M | x | | | | | | |
| Milk | M | x | | | | | | |
| Fruit drink | M | x | x | x | x | x | x | x |
| Melba toast | M | x | x | | | x | | |
| Beef jerky | S | x | | x | | x | x | x |
| Trail cookies | S | x | | x | x | x | x | x |
| Tropical chocolate bars | S | x | | x | | x | x | x |
| Beef hash | S | x | | | | | | |
| Corn | S | x | | | | | | |
| Peas | S | x | | | | | | |
| Pudding | S | x | | | | | | x |
| Cocoa | M | x | xx | x | x | x | xx | xx |
| Scrambled eggs | S | | x | | x | | | x |
| Peanut butter & jelly sand. | S | | x | | | | | |
| Vanilla shake mix | S | | x | | | | | |
| Beef noodle soup | M | | x | | | x | | |
| Chili-mac w/beef | S | | x | | | | | |
| Green beans | S | | x | | | | | |
| Apple compote | S | | x | | x | | | |
| Fruit cocktail | S | | | x | | | | |
| French toast | S | | | x | | | x | |
| Chicken & noodles | M | | | x | | | | |
| Pudding w/raisins | S | | | x | | | | |
| Bacon (dried) | S | | | | x | | | x |
| Hash-brown potatoes | M | | | | x | | | x |
| Swiss chese w/bacon sand. | S | | | | x | | | |
| Chocolate shake mix | S | | | | x | | | |
| Ham chedderton | M | | | | x | | | |
| Instant oatmeal | S | | | | | x | | |
| Instant breakfast | M | | | | | x | | |
| Chip beef on rice | M | | | | | x | | |
| Gravy | M | | | | | x | | |
| Applesauce | S | | | | | x | | |
| Strawberry shake mix | S | | | | | | x | |
| Beef stroganoff | M | | | | | | x | |
| Choc. pudding | S | | | | | | x | |
| Punch | M | | | | | | | x |
| Turkey & rice | M | | | | | | | x |

M-Supermarket          S-Specialty Shop

# Breakfast

**CAMP BREAKFASTS**

Orange juice
Cold cereal
Boiled eggs
Toast and butter
Milk

Grapefruit juice
Cold cereal
Toast and butter
Milk

Blended fruit juice
Oatmeal
Brown sugar
Toast and butter
Milk

Tomato juice
Banana pancakes
Cereal
Syrup
Bread and butter
Cocoa
Milk

Sliced oranges
French toast
Bread and butter
Cereal
Syrup or jam
Cocoa
Milk

Orange juice
Hot cereal
Bacon
Toast and butter
Milk

Pineapple juice
Cereal
Scrambled eggs
Bread and butter
Jam
Cocoa
Milk

Blended juice
Cold cereal
Corn muffins and butter
Milk

Stewed prunes
Cereal
Fried eggs
Bread and butter
Jam
Cocoa
Milk

**TRAIL BREAKFASTS**
  (Use nonrefrigerated food)

Stewed or dried prunes
Quick oats
Pancakes with camp-made syrup
Hot chocolate

Stewed peaches
Cornmeal mush
French toast with jam
Hot chocolate

Quick oats with raisins
Grilled bacon
Hot biscuits with jelly
Hot chocolate

# Lunch

## CAMP LUNCHES

Canned meat and lettuce sandwiches
Peanut butter and jelly sandwiches
Applesauce
Milk

Macaroni and cheese
Carrot strips
Fig bars
Milk

Hamburgers
Pickles
Potato chips
Bread
Catsup
Fruit drink or milk

Fried canned meat and syrup
Green beans
Bread and butter
Butterscotch pudding
Milk

Tomato-vegetable soup
Egg and relish or cheese sandwiches
Oatmeal cookies
Chocolate milk

Salmon and egg sandwiches
Lettuce and tomato salad
Bread and butter
Canned plums
Milk

Baked beans
Hot dogs
Catsup
Bread and butter
Sliced peaches
Milk

French onion soup
Peanut butter and jam sandwiches
Carrot sticks
Chocolate pudding
Chocolate milk

## TRAIL LUNCHES

Peanut butter sandwich
Jam sandwich
Carrot sticks
Butterscotch pudding
Instant fruit drink

Cheese or luncheon meat sandwiches
Raisins
Apple
Instant fruit drink

Corned beef or apple butter
    sandwiches
Dates
Instant fruit drink

Cheese sandwiches
Sliced tomato salad
Bread and butter
Cupcakes
Milk

## BIRD SEED MIX

Sugared cereal
Candy-coated chocolate
Raisins
Unsalted nuts

Dinner

## CAMP DINNERS

Salisbury steak
Boiled potatoes
Corn
Fresh fruit salad
Rolls and butter
Vanilla pudding
Milk

Macaroni and cheese
Grilled Spam
Beef bouillon
Fresh carrots
Rice pudding
Chocolate milk

Ham slice with pineapple
Potatoes
Corn
Butterscotch pudding
Bread and butter
Milk

Corn beef hash
Potatoes
Onions
Peas
Bread and butter
Sliced peaches
Milk

Noodle soup
Salmon cakes
Boiled potatoes
Buttered beans
Bread and butter
Cake with fruit sauce
Milk

Chicken and gravy
Rice
Peas
Biscuits
Bread pudding
Milk

Split pea soup
Beef and gravy
Potatoes and onions
Corn and carrots
Bread and butter
Vanilla pudding
Milk

French onion soup
Fried chicken leg
Baked potato
Peas and carrots
Biscuits with butter
Baked apples
Milk

## ONE-POT DINNERS

Quick Irish stew with vegetables
Bread and butter
Apple Betty
Milk
Fruit drink

Beef stew
Lettuce and tomato salad
Bread and butter
Fresh fruit
Milk

## TRAIL DINNERS

Split pea soup
Creamed chipped beef on biscuits
Corn and lima beans
Peach cobbler (in foil)
Milk

Beef bouillon
Spaghetti and meatballs
Peas and carrots
Corn muffins
Chocolate pudding
Milk

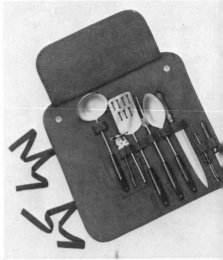

Your cooking tools may include a compact kit, shown above, and an aluminum Dutch oven that can be used to cook or bake, shown on the left.

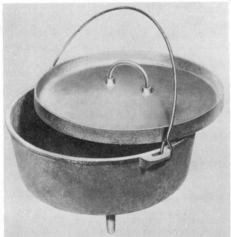

A Scout Trail Chief cook kit contains nearly all the utensils you will need.

Whether you make a delicious meal for solo consumption, work more elaborately to prepare food for yourself and five or six others to pass a test, or undertake the bigger job of chief cook for a camp; the basic utensils with which you'll do the cooking remain the same. Their size will vary with the size of the job, of course, as will the amounts of food that you'll plan for.

Instead of making lists of the great quantities of utensils from which you (the outdoor cook) may choose, let's concentrate on some of the basic items.

Pots, pans, dishes, and tableware from home will often do very nicely. When you cook outdoors alone, the minimum equipment will be two small kettles with covers and bails, a skillet (a folding or detachable handle is a good feature), tablespoon, fork, and a cup that won't scorch your lips as you try to sip a hot drink. You'll find it handy to use your skillet as a plate; the cup will do double-duty as a bowl.

## Carry a Fair Share

On a patrol hike where eating's involved, remember that each Scout carries his own utensils — usually a bowl-plate, cup, knife, fork, and spoon will do the job. Each Scout also carries his share of bigger pots. Here's the reason: If one Scout carries the entire nest of pots, pans, and plates, he'll end up with more than he can conveniently carry. A good way of being more systematic about the situation is to "break the pots down" so that the tops of several packs will hold the different units. Then, foods that are crushable can be carried inside the pots and will be protected during the journey.

The second thing to remember for timesaving is this: Plan things so that packages for each individual meal are kept together. Keep a record of which pack holds each meal, and it won't be necessary to dig into more than one pack when hunger pangs are hammering at your insides.

## More About Your Gear

Lightness is important, to be sure. So is toughness and the ability to take hard use for a long time. The Boy Scout aluminum pots are designed to fill these camper's needs. Of course, it is possible to buy less-expensive cooking kits, but the experienced trail man will tell you that the flimsiness of such utensils lessens their efficiency in holding heat. Open air tends to cool food very quickly, and this fact alone is a strong argument against using gear that is too light. Also, in order to cut the cost of these kits, it is necessary to cut the quality.

The skillet or frying pan is a very helpful utensil for cooking over (or before) an open fire. Use this utensil for bannock, pancakes, thick soups, meats, potatoes—or even for stews or quick desserts. You can count on this helper when you really want to travel light.

# Hot Tips About Fires

There's an important difference —a "new look"—in the way the wise Scout prepares a base for his fire.

If they dig pits for fires, several patrols on a cookout can unconsciously work together to leave the place looking like a shell-torn battlefield.

So, now the word about the base for the fire is "build up, don't dig down."

The requirements point out that soil used to raise a platform for your fire should be at least 2 inches deep, and of "unburnable soil." What this means simply is that you should avoid leaf mold, pine needles, mosses, or other materials that will burn instead of insulate your fire site — with consequent damage to plantlife beneath it.

The way to build your fire base is to do it as you dig your latrine. That is, when digging your latrine, simply use your plastic sheet to carry part of the soil to your fire spot. Build a flat-topped mound 3 or 4 inches high, and 3 or 4 feet in diameter. This allows plenty of room for the fire, and you'll have additional room for utensils. As a bonus, you will find that the raised loose dirt will help you to level the rocks that support your pots or grill.

Camp cooks who've tried it find that two loads of dirt, easily carried in the plastic cloth, can be brought to where it's needed, leveled, and tamped, all in about 7 minutes.

## Five Rules for Fire Building

Let's review the five simple steps followed by the successful fire builder.

1. Put your fireplace in a spot from which fire will not spread. To be sure, clear combustible materials from 6 to 8 feet away from the hot spot. Check the area for overhanging branches.

2. Have all materials for your fire within reach before lighting up. This means tinder, kindling, and fuel.

3. Place your tinder next to a log or tin can pointed toward the wind. This will offer support to your kindling (and firewood) until it is well lighted and going strong.

4. Light your tinder on the windward side, then shield the infant fire from the wind until the flame catches and spreads.

5. Feed the fire — gently at first, then nourish its growing appetite as needed. Don't try to force things; you'll just have to start over again if the first effort is smothered.

## What Wood To Use

Squaw woods (an Indian name for small dead branches that a squaw could gather) from evergreens are good fire starters, poor choices for cooking. The pitch that lets these woods ignite quickly also results in smoking, popping, and soot. These

Make your fire to fit your situation. Above are the rock fireplace, slab, and tepee fire setups. Below is the crisscross type.

play havoc with the careful timing a cook can expect from woods that burn down well to good coals.

Dead evergreen twigs and branches are easy to gather in many places; many live evergreen trees have lower branches that are dead and brittle. At the same time, the upper foliage protects your kindling from moisture during rainy weather.

Another first-rate kindling is the bark peeled from dead birch trees. Its pitch content is reasonably high, and the bark is thin and curly enough to be easily crushed into a tinder.

Regardless of what you use for your tinder and kindling, let's emphasize again starting your fire small with just enough open space for oxygen to circulate until the fire is burning. Then add larger pieces of wood, to finger-thickness.

Standing dead hardwood trees are generally the best source of wood for your cooking fires. In contrast to your pitchy kindlings, such woods as hickory, maple, oak, apple, or beech reduce to long-lasting coals, without too much "pop" or smoke. We say "standing" hardwoods because deadfalls or branches often have rotted — or absorbed so much moisture that they are not good firewood at all.

Whatever your choice of available wood, be sure to pile a good supply of well-split firewood near the fire. This way you can concentrate on your main job of cooking without having to find another stick or two of fuel when you need it.

## Some Undesirable Woods

Popping, sparking, and excessive smoke are three undesirable qualities to be avoided in your choice of firewood. Some woods have rather odd odors that can spoil the flavor of your food, too. Here are a few to put on your "unwanted" list—for one or more of the reasons listed: basswood, chestnut, box elder, sassafras, tamarack, tulip, white elm, and willow.

## Wet Weather Fire Building

We hope that all of your outdoor cooking will find the smoke of your fire straight and tall, into clear skies. But such wishful thinking can't eliminate the fact of dampness. If you're not prepared for rain, the test of your cooking skill isn't likely to be a successful one. Perhaps these tips can save you from eating cold canned soup when a hot and delicious meal is rightfully yours.

For wet weather kindling, take advantage of your skill with an ax to whack away at the sheltered side of a dead stump or standing dead tree. The inside part will be dry, and even the side away from the rain will furnish some good kindling.

Thousands of acres of woodlands burn every year, because someone failed to put out a fire thoroughly. First extinguish your fire by sprinkling it with water. Splash the water on with your hand since a spray is much more effective than a solid stream of water. Turn smoldering sticks and logs over and continue using water until only soaking wet ashes remain. Bury wet ashes in your latrine or cover the spot with dirt.

# Grills

We know the green logs or well-placed granite rocks are handy rests for our pots and pans and that a well-built fireplace is a handy gadget to have around the fire, but we won't always find that these things are easy to come by. In such cases, the portable wire grill is a real timesaver. It's possible to buy almost any kind of grill on which you can broil meats and fish to a sizzling, well-browned doneness that makes your mouth water just to think about it.

The wisdom that's earned by an aching back, though, dictates that the simplest forms of the grill to be carried along on your trip are the best. Leave the more elaborate jobs for the patio or permanent camp.

A wire rack fitted with folding wire legs that can be forced into the ground is a good kind and doesn't take too much room in your pack. Or, use three wire tent pegs. Simply poke them into the ground in a rough circle large enough to provide stability for your cooking utensil, yet small enough to ensure you that an accidental nudge of a pot handle won't drop part of your meal into the fire.

Equally simple pot supports are fire racks or metal rods to be supported by the explosion-proof rocks which you'll choose to contain your fire.

Don't try to move the fire under the fly. It will smoke like the dickens and drive you out into the rain.

Some states now require that all fires in public parks be built in an enclosed fireplace. And, supplies of natural firewood have been so depleted by unwise use that it's sometimes necessary to pack in your fuel. Solution to the firewood problem is taking a supply of charcoal or charcoal briquettes.

## Using Charcoal

It takes practice to use charcoal effectively for cooking. You can do a fine job with it, once you learn how it behaves.

In the first place, never use flammable liquids to start a charcoal fire. For one thing, they burn off fast, often without getting the fuel well lighted, especially if it's charcoal. Then there is that often fatal tendency to pour on more liquid and—boom!

Even with charcoal briquettes, use twigs and squaw-wood fragments, plus plenty of draft, to give you a sure, safe start. Always allow about $\frac{1}{2}$ hour extra to give your charcoal fire time to reach a steady, smokeless glow for clean, powerful heat.

## SOME CHARCOAL TIPS

Know how much charcoal you will need for the cooking job that is to be done.

Let a new fire get started for at least 10 to 15 minutes before you start to cook over it.

You can temper the heat if it gets too brisk by sprinkling a few drops of water on the fuel.

For quickest cooking, put your utensil close to the coals. Be sure to leave space for adequate draft.

Kill your fire just as soon as you've finished with it by dousing it with water. You can let the sun dry out the remaining charcoal to be used another time.

25

Foldaway Charcoal Grill

# Keep It Clean

One of the principles most basic to Scouting is the one which states, "Leave your campsite neater than it was when you first saw it."

Without preaching at all, there's another good healthy reason for good sanitation and cleanup practice while you're traveling on the trail or in camp. We have read too many times about cases of food poisoning. You've probably suffered from diarrhea at one time or another—and no matter what the cause, you remember the ailment as both weakening and unpleasant.

In short, keep yourself and your food (and its containers) clean. Otherwise, you risk spoiling a cooking experience that could have been totally good.

One of the important rules of

outdoor cooking is "ready availability of plenty of hot water." This means that you have at least one large potful on the fire before you sit to eat!

## Disposal of Trash and Garbage

"Dig" has been a word associated with camping for generations. Outdoorsmen have dug hip-holes for a comfortable, woodsy bed. We have been taught to dig a base for a fire, to dig holes for burial of trash and garbage. But now, after seeing aftereffects of such digging in our dwindling wilderness areas, conservationists and Scouts have agreed that a great deal of digging has led to a type of destruction of its own—even while intentions were the best.

Digging destroys plantlife. And, several patrols gathered for a friendly and satisfying overnight camp can leave a site looking rather "shell shocked" with raw dirt covering fire sites, latrines, garbage disposal spots, and dishwater pits.

At the same time, the well-known animal habit of digging is encouraged when we bury used cans, food scraps, or wrappings.

Wild animal noses are fantastically sensitive to food odors. It's a part of the law of survival that leads to frantic digging-up of anything we leave behind in the way of cans, bottles, foil, or food scraps.

Even with burned garbage, the word now is "don't bury it — carry it out." That's because any other way tempts wildlife to scatter unattractive trash and create a dangerous eyesore all over the landscape.

This precaution is just as appropriate to New England is it is to the Far West. It's not only the larger animals (bears, for example) that dig. Raccoons, foxes, porcupines, and skunks are offenders, too. Even the slow armadillo can scatter aluminum foil over a wide area after he's pawed through 2 feet of dirt in search of buried material.

The substitute method? Pack a tote-litter bag with you to use for carrying out any materials you don't (or can't) burn.

# Dishwashing

Dishwashing can be less of a chore if it is done skillfully, with Scouts sharing the responsibilities. The safe, quick way to wash dishes is shown here.

**CLEANUP SCOUTS DO THIS**

**1.** Start with full pot of boiling water. Use some for washing and remainder for rinsing.

**2.** Mix part of boiling water with liquid soap and cold water for washing.

**3.** Add sanitizing agent to the remaining hot water for rinse water.

**4.** While other Scouts wash their utensils, cleanup Scouts begin cleaning cooking pots.

## PATROL DISHWASHING EQUIPMENT

Two large pots—one for rinsing
(6 to 8 qt.), one for washing
(4 to 6 qt.)
One plastic dish swab
Liquid soap in plastic container
Chemical sanitizing agent
Two or three scouring pads
Dunking equipment (tongs or bag)
One plastic sheet, 4 by 4 feet
Water container
Roll of paper towels

## OTHER SCOUTS DO THIS

**5.** Each Scout wipes off his own eating utensils.

**6.** Then he washes them in pot of wash water.

**7.** Now he rinses and sterilizes utensils by dunking them in pot of rinse water.

**8.** Finally, he air-dries utensils by placing them on a plastic sheet. Store in flyproof container.

29

# Steps in Making Tote-Litter Bag.

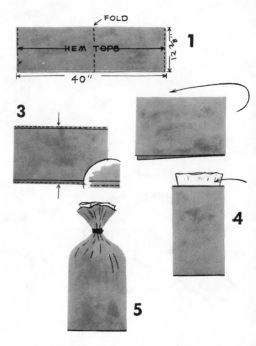

**FOLD**

**HEM TOPS**

**1**

12 3/8"

40"

**3**

**4**

**5**

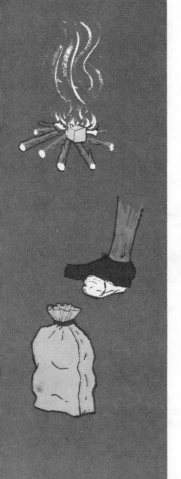

## The Tote-Litter Bag

A tote-litter bag is a canvas bag lined with a disposable plastic bag so it won't leak. Its share of room in your inbound pack is quite small. And your outbound hike isn't overburdened with either bulk or weight, because the trash and garbage in the tote-litter bag is a lighter substitute for the food packed in. Supervisors and rangers in parks across the Nation are enthusiastic about this practice. These experts in outdoor living recommend that unburnables be carried to the nearest recognized trash dis-

posal — or all the way to y[...] home, if necessary.

Sealing the bag is simp[...] Use a rubber band or tw[...] sealer. Either is reusable, [...] the plastic-covered wire sea[...] is probably more durable a[...] dependable.

*Once more for emphasis: Do[...] bury garbage or trash. Carry[...] out.* The only material t[...] should be buried is ashes fr[...] your campfire when you co[...] the latrine trench and prep[...] to expose once more the grou[...] you covered for your fire p[...] form in the first place.

# Cooking Terms

As your knowledge of cooking grows, you'll be understood pretty well if you use a few basic terms to describe what you intend to do to your food. It might be a point of pride, too, to be able to instruct Scouts in your patrol when your leader asks you to tell them what you have learned.

Here are a few basic terms:

BAKE.—To cook by dry heat, as in a reflector oven or Dutch oven.

BASTE. — To moisten cooking food with melted fat, drippings, or specially mixed sauces, such as barbecue sauce.

BOIL.—To cook in water—or liquid that's mostly water—at boiling temperature. Bubbles will keep rising to the surface and break there.

BRAISE.—To brown in fat, then cook in covered pan with or without added liquid.

BROIL.—To cook uncovered, over direct heat over an open fire.

FRY.—To cook in fat.

MARINATE.—Treatment of food (usually meat) by letting it stand in a liquid to add flavor or to tenderize.

PLANK.—To cook and serve on wooden slab or board.

POACH. — Cook below boiling point in water or other liquid that covers the food.

ROAST. — To bake in hot air, without water or cover.

SAUTÉ. — To fry lightly and quickly in a little hot fat.

SCALD. — Heat to temperature just below the boiling point.

SEAR.—Sealing of surface by exposing it to intense heat.

SIMMER.—Cook in hot liquid at temperature just below the boiling point.

STEEP.—Extract flavor and nutritive value by soaking in water that is hot but not boiling.

STEW.—To boil or simmer in a small amount of liquid.

TOAST.—To brown by dry heat.

# Camp and Trail Recipes

Most cooks have a favorite recipe or a dozen of them. Some have been borrowed from friends, others from one of the sources of cookbooks published every year. Still others have been handed down through generations, or are the product of an inventive mind when a bunch of ingredients had to be put together in a hurry to feed unexpected guests.

Wherever recipes come from, getting them together is usually easier than keeping them so that they're readable, filed in order—or even in a place where you can find them in time, every time.

Among the other sources for good recipes, see your *Scout Handbook*.

## CHILI BURGER STEAK

To serve four men or two boys, you'll need:

**1 lb. fresh ground chuck or hamburger**
**10 to 15 drops of cooking oil or ½ pat of butter**
**1 can of chili beef soup**
**Salt, pepper, chili powder**

Preheat pan or pot to medium warmth over coals. Oil the utensil, then flatten your meat to 1-inch thickness (about as thick as the width of your first two fingers). Brown for 5 minutes, turn over, and let the other side brown thoroughly.

Cover utensil while you open soup, dilute contents with half a can of water, pour over meat. Cover again and set to back of the fire for another 2 or 3 minutes. Extra chili powder is for the ones who like a little additional "heat."

## SKILLET BREAD

This bannock is simple to mix if you prefer to get away from the prepared biscuit mix once in a while. Serves four people.

**1 cup flour**
**1 tsp. baking powder**
**1 cup water**
**3 tbsp. salad oil**
**½ tsp. salt**

Mix and sift dry ingredients. Mix with just enough water (with oil added) to form a stiff dough. Dust your hands with some of the flour, and make a round flat cake—with as few motions as possible. Dust the dough with a little more flour, set it into prewarmed skillet or baking tin. Bake on the coals, propped in front of the fire, or in reflector oven. (Note: it's often easier to use a prepared biscuit mix. This recipe is included for the cook who wants to know how to do the job from scratch.)

## FISH CHOWDER

**4 strips of sliced bacon (from slab) or ½ lb. salt pork, diced**

**1 medium onion, chopped**

**2 or 3 potatoes, diced or chopped**

**3 cups water**

**1 lb. of fish chunks, without skin or bones**

**1 pint milk or 1 cup evaporated milk**

**1 tsp. celery salt**

**1 tsp. of blended dried herbs or same amount of mixed thyme and savory**

**½ tsp. salt**

**½ tsp. pepper**

Fry diced bacon or pork until crisp. Dry on paper towel (or even newspaper) while you lightly fry onion in grease. Add potatoes and water, boil slowly until nearly done.

Add remaining ingredients and simmer for 15 minutes, or until the fish is done.

The herbs are not vital, but add to the delicious flavor.

## DINNER IN A POT

(Feel free to substitute ingredients in this recipe.)

**3 tbsp. bacon fat, cooking oil, or shortening**

**1 medium onion, sliced**

**1 lb. ground beef**

**1 green pepper**

**Beans**

**Corn kernels cut from four or five ears**

**1 tsp. garlic salt**

**½ tsp. black pepper**

**½ tsp. dried sage (if you want it)**

With hot fat in skillet, sauté sliced onion until tender. Remove onion, leave hot fat. "Scramble the hamburger" by breaking it into small pieces, brown it slowly. Pour off fat when meat is light brown, then add the onion, the slices of green pepper, beans, and corn. Add garlic salt and pepper; and your choice of herbs; simmer until done (green pepper will be tender).

## BASIC GRAVY

**Gravy made from drippings you'll gather from roasted meat needs only salt and pepper for seasoning. Skim off most of the fat, add necessary seasoning, and serve.**

If amount of juices and drippings is small, add some water. You can add flavor with a bouillon cube or two, meat-based soups, or cooked vegetables such as peas, carrots, or onions.

## BEEF STEW

(serves eight)

Utensils needed for this meal include: frying pan, 2-quart kettle, measuring cup, measuring spoon, spatula, Dutch oven, paring knife (2 if available), pan for washing vegetables, and a large spoon.

**3 lbs. stewing beef cut into
2-inch cubes
Shortening
½ cup flour
½ tsp. salt
¼ tsp. pepper
8 small onions
8 medium carrots
8 medium potatoes**

To prepare this meal, do the following:

1. Put about 3 tablespoons of shortening in frying pan and put on coals to heat.
2. Put 2-quart kettle, half filled with water, on coals to heat.
3. Mix ½ cup flour, ½ teaspoon salt, and ¼ teaspoon pepper together.
4. Rub meat in flour mixture, doing a few pieces at a time.
5. When frying pan is *hot*, start to brown meat. Do not overload pan. Browning will take place only when meat surface is in contact with the bottom of the pan. Add more shortening as needed. Brown all sides thoroughly. As pieces are browned, remove them and place in Dutch oven. Do not pierce meat as you turn or take pieces out. You want juices sealed in.
6. Remove ends and outer layer from *one* onion. Dice into small pieces about ¼-inch square. Brown in frying pan and then put in Dutch oven. This can be done with the meat.
7. When last meat and onions have been removed from frying pan, put about 2 cups of hot water in frying pan and bring to a boil. Scrape bottom of pan with spatula and then pour contents over meat.
8. Add additional hot water to cover meat and put lid on. Place Dutch oven on coals. Cook over low heat for at least 2½ hours. It should be *simmering* at all times. Check every 20 to 30 minutes. Adjust heat if necessary. Add hot water as needed.
9. One hour before you expect to eat:
a. Peel potatoes; wash in cold

water; cut in 1-inch cubes.

b.  Remove ends and outer layers of onions; cut into fourths.

c.  Scrape carrots; remove ends; wash and cut in ½-inch slices.

d.  Put all vegetables into Dutch oven, add hot water to cover vegetables, and put on lid.

10.  Simmer until vegetables are tender, stirring occasionally to make sure stew is not sticking to bottom.

Allow at least 3 hours to cook. In camp, start meat at noon and let it simmer all afternoon, checking it occasionally.

## STUFFED BAKED FISH
### (serves 6)
**1 dressed fish, about 5 pounds**
**1 rounded tsp. salt**
**4 tbsp. melted butter or other fat**
**3 or 4 slices bacon**

Rub inside and outside of fish with salt. Stuff fish loosely, fasten with skewers or sew body cavity shut. Grease pan, brush fish with melted fat. Drape bacon over fish. Bake in oven at temperature of 350° for about 12 minutes per pound of fish.

Serve on hot dishes, if possible.

Stuffing is made with chopped onion, bread crumbs, melted fat, salt, dash of pepper, and your choice of herbs that are good with fish. Use about 2 cups bread crumbs; add other ingredients to taste. Keep the stuffing on the dry side, but use a little water to mix.

## QUICK BOSTON BAKED BEANS
### (serves 8 persons)

Utensils needed for this old favorite are: No. 10 Dutch oven, can opener, measuring cup, spoon for stirring, paring knife.

**2 1-lb. cans baked beans**
**¼ cup brown sugar**
**¼ cup catsup**
**1 small onion**
**2 slices bacon**

To prepare, do the following:

1.  Open beans and put contents in Dutch oven. Remove pork.

2.  Put ¼ cup of brown sugar on beans.

3.  Add ¼ cup of catsup to beans.

4.  Add ½ cup of water to beans and stir gently with spoon.

5.  Cut off ends and remove outer layer from onion. Cut onion in quarters and put on top of beans.

6.  Cut 2 slices of bacon in half and put on beans. Put lid on.

7.  Set Dutch oven over 9 to 12 briquettes and put about the same number on lid. Bring liquid to a simmer and keep it simmering for about an hour.

Figure on this taking a little over 1 hour to cook this meal.

## FRENCH TOAST

(This is enough for two. For extra servings, add milk to batter and use extra bread.)

**4 eggs (or reconstituted powdered eggs)**
**¼ cup reconstituted dry milk**
**6 slices bread (white or whole wheat)**
**¼ tsp. salt**

Beat eggs, milk, and salt until thoroughly blended. Dip slices of bread in the mixture, letting them soak up the batter. Fry in a lightly greased skillet over moderately high heat until golden brown on both sides. Serve with syrup, jam, or jelly.

## SCRAMBLED EGGS

**2 or 3 eggs in shell**
**¼ tsp. salt**
**Pinch of thyme**
**Black pepper to taste**

Have skillet warm, with very light coating of grease. Break eggs into separate dish with salt and other flavorings, beat well with a fork until eggs are frothy. Do not add milk, but stir eggs with fork as they cook — just enough to gather the steaming eggs into a light portion about the size of your palm. Serve on hot plate if possible.

## SOURDOUGH BISCUITS

**1 cup sourdough starter**
(See "Breads and Biscuits" section of this pamphlet for the starter recipe)
**¼ tsp. baking soda**
**1 egg (or equivalent egg powder)**
**1 tbsp. melted fat**
**Enough flour to make a stiff dough**

Mix ingredients until they're blended into a dough that you're able to knead. Roll dough flat on a floured surface such as foil, plastic, or a smooth board. Cut dough into biscuit-sized pieces. Let rise for an hour or so, if possible, then bake until golden brown in your Dutch oven, reflector baker, or use a greased skillet before the fire.

# LET'S GET COOKING!

## Vegetables and Salads

Your clip-out recipes show interesting ways in which vegetables can be combined with meats, fish, and other things to make combination dishes. Every man has his favorite. You're lucky enough to be able to add the spice of outdoors to vegetables that you cook, and that's a very special advantage. On trips that take you days away from refrigeration, your selection of vegetables will be limited to those that may be canned, dehydrated, or freeze-dried, or that are dried as they ripen in the field.

There are bottled salad dressings available that don't need to be kept cool. Even more convenient are the new dehydrated salad dressings (including blue cheese, garlic cheese, French, and Russian), packed in sealed foil envelopes and needing only addition of water and vinegar before flavoring your greens.

## Sweets

Our bodies practically holler for sweets and fats while working harder away from the daily routine, so the subject of desserts is important. If you're out in the wilderness for a considerable length of time, you'll find yourself getting thin and tough — even though you eat twice as much as you might at home.

So! Dried fruits, puddings, chocolate, and hard candy are needed and convenient. With your reflector oven or Dutch oven, you can make gingerbread, coffeecake, apple Betty, several kinds of pies. Your biscuits or bannock will combine with fresh or preserved fruits for excellent shortcakes.

## Eggs and Cheeses

Scrambled dehydrated eggs properly prepared add variety to any meal of the day. Save breakage of fresh eggs by breaking them before you start the trip. Use a plastic container (sealed with tape), or one plastic bag tucked inside another as a carrier. Another way to prevent premature and messy breakage is to hardboil the eggs before starting.

*Hard* cheeses are the ones an outdoor cook prefers. They keep well. Try grated Parmesan, or cheddar that is not too moist. Swiss cheese will keep well only if it's kept wrapped and cool.

**FRYING EGGS.** "Sunny-side up" eggs are the simplest to make. Melt a teaspoon of margarine or bacon fat to grease the entire pan. Break eggs into the pan before it smokes much. As it fries gently, baste the yolk with hot fat. Continue to fry until the white is firm, but do not overcook.

Breakfast is one meal that is too easily neglected at home, either in the hurry of getting to school, or skipped entirely on holidays. But in camp or on the trail, so much energy is required for hiking, swimming, or running that breakfast becomes a necessity as well as a pleasure.

There is no bugle call like the smell of bacon and eggs to get you out of the sack. And once your troop or patrol gets its breakfast appetite sharpened, the cooks have to be on the job early. But once the fire is ready and all the ingredients are lined up, morning cookery isn't difficult. A few helpful hints to make it still easier are on the following pages.

**MAKING PANCAKES.** A prepared mix can be used according to the instructions on the package. The pan should be heated until a drop of water will "dance" for 3 seconds. Grease lightly. Pour batter. When bubbles form the pancake is ready to be turned.

**MAKING OATMEAL.** Individual packages of oatmeal are now available. Prepare by placing contents in bowl and adding boiling water according to directions.

For a change sometime, you might try this way of coddling eggs. Clean the segments from half an orange skin or cut a large onion in half and remove all but about the three outer layers. Crack an egg into the shell and set it in the coals to cook the usual time. When done, eat it right from the container—after removing the scorched onion layer, you can even eat the container! Onions have vitamin C, too.

In some circumstances, you can try novel ways of cooking without utensils that actually add to the flavor and enjoyment of eating. This type of originality is particularly good when you are carrying minimum equipment.

Breakfast is one meal that lends itself especially well to compact, quick preparation. It does not take much effort to peel an orange, boil a few prunes, open a can of juice or a box of cereal, or to make a few pieces of toast near the fire.

**HOT PIE.** A reflector oven that lets you see what is going on and permits adjustment of baking condition makes fresh berry pie and many other things possible at camp.

# The Reflector Oven

A cook who doesn't care who's hurt by flying puns could say the reflector baker is a way to add bounce to cooking. Well, that's exactly what a reflector does for food inside it—bounces heat from the fire to the spot where it will do the most good, whether your menu calls for baking of breads, meats, pies, cakes, biscuits, or other foods. The most common reflector is the folding kind that can be broken down and set up in a matter of minutes. Remember that aluminum foil (the heavier type) can be used for the same purpose as a temporary oven. It will reflect heat rays to the top of your dish —and brown it while the basic cooking of that dish comes from below and behind.

Incidentally, here we depart from the standard recommendation that "coals make the best cooking fire." For reflector baking and cooking, the ideal fire is the one that's moderately high and blazing so that heat is thrown into the slanting top and bottom of the baker. Regulation of temperature is done simply by moving the reflector toward the fire or away from it.

Make pastry dough right in the baking pan: Use a mix and make half quantity for the bottom; gently pat dough thinly over pan. Or use piecrust recipe; divide in two, and roll out bottom crust.

Now fill crust with washed, culled and hulled berries. To a pint of berries add ½ cup of sugar, 2 tablespoons of flour, and a dash of cinnamon, if you like. (Be sure to bring some along if it's berry season, for goodness' sake! After all, you brought the oven.)

Mix the other half of your pastry on a sheet of foil, lightly floured, and pat it out with floured hands (or roll it) to ⅛-inch thickness, an inch wider than the pan. Keep it uniform and avoid patching, if possible. An aluminum tent-pole section makes a pretty good rolling pin. Keep it clean.

Flip the whole business over on top of the pie, centering it carefully on the pie. Now peel back the foil from the crust, and trim and crimp the edges to seal it off. Slash the crust to vent the steam, or prick it here and there with a fork if you'd rather.

Put your pies (why stop at one?) on the oven shelf. Build up your fire; you're using reflected heat, so keep that fire bright. Keep an eye out for scorching, and turn occasionally.

47

# The Gourmet Touch

Men who have cooked outdoors for years, having been trained in the art as Scouts, have never lost the feeling of fun and accomplishment that comes when they prepare a satisfying meal. One of the fine points they have picked up over the years is the use of seasoning besides salt and pepper.

Many herbs for cooking, including basil, marjoram, parsley, savory, and thyme can be used to flavor nearly any food—from scrambled eggs to roasts.

*Caution:* don't use much of any herb in cooking. It's the subtle hint, rather than a solid right cross to the palate that distinguishes the experienced cook from the heavy-handed amateur.

Dried herbs are three or four times as potent as the same measure of green herbs.

Before taking any herbs along on a hike or camping expedition, it would be well to get advice from an expert cook. Some of these flavoring agents are mixed with the food before cooking, while others are added afterward. Some are so potent that it is sufficient to rub them in the cooking utensil or on the food itself. There is no doubt that skillful use of herbs is a mark of an excellent chef and distinctive touch to your outdoor meals.

# Dry, Dried, and Nonrefrigerated Foods

Dried foods have been part of the American diet since pioneer days. The need for rations along wilderness paths used by traders and explorers—even the homesteader's cabin on the prairie—offered no chance for refrigeration. So foods were salted, air-dried, parched by fire, or smoked for preservation.

"Pemmican" and "jerky" were meat-based foods, as were various hams and sausages heavily charged with dry salt or brine before they were smoked over smoldering beds of hickory wood or corncobs. We have excellent dried or cured meats today.

You can't beat dehydrated foods for a backpack outing.

They're lightweight, compact, easy to carry and prepare, don't spoil, and they're nourishing and tasty. They're all handled the same way, whether they're freeze-dried, conventionally dehydrated, or air-dried. However, the types of food you choose and how and where you buy them can affect your pocketbook and the overall success of your outing.

The two prime sources of dehydrated foods are local markets and special stores catering to campers and hikers. Items such as dried eggs are found only in specialty shops. But most supermarkets have a surprisingly large selection and, on a majority of products, you can shop and choose.

Careful shopping can save you money. Most of the big markets and some special stores, even discount houses, give discounts to groups. Ask the manager. Even some wholesale houses will

cooperate on large purchases. Bulk buying and repackaging to your own needs in plastic bags is worth the effort on selected foods.

When prices are comparable, your best bet is the supermarkets where competition has forced producers to give greater thought to taste and ease of preparation than in the specialty area. For a complete menu, however, you'll probably have to divide your purchases between the two stores.

Dried or packaged soups are examples of popular supermarket items. Several companies offer a wide selection of soups conveniently packaged in small amounts. Chunks of real beef, chicken, or other tasty morsels add body to the broth.

Dehydrated shoestring potatoes and hash-browns have few equals. Not only do they smell tempting and taste delicious, but they require no soaking. You put the potatoes in a pan, add the right amount of water, and heat. When the water is gone and the food is hot, you're ready to eat.

A newly developed product, the "retort" pouch, is now available. Containing primarily main dishes, these lightweight, compact pouches need no refrigeration and have a long shelf life. These flexible packages also are easy to prepare—just drop them in boiling water for the time listed on the instructions.

## Bulky Food

Melba toast is about the bulkiest item you'll want to pack.

It keeps well, comes in a variety of types (cinnamon is one), and has many uses. The boys can heat it over the fire, make French toast of it, dip it in hot cocoa, or break it up for soup croutons.

Many brands of cocoa rate high with campers. However, you can mix your own by this little-known but economical recipe used for many years on the Northern Wisconsin National High Adventure Base: 1lb. cocoa, 2 lbs. dried milk, 3 lbs. sugar, equals 6 lbs. cocoa mix. If you buy individually packed servings, expect to pay more money.

The array of dried fruits has increased into a pleasant variety over the years, too. The assortment includes raisins, apricots, prunes, peaches, and pears—along with dried apples, which make a good sauce or pie when the camp cook takes time to prepare them. On-the-trail snacks of edible dried fruits are unfailing sources of quick blood sugar to help restore pep when the going gets rough.

## Variety and Light Weight

Whether you are heading for a day's outing climbing the high mountains with a pack on your back or are on a long canoe expedition or overnight hike, the convenience or light weight of many foods can increase your efficiency—and your fun.

Modern lightweight foods are classified as dried, dehydrated, concentrated, or freeze-dried. The distinctions overlap a bit and are largely technical anyhow. The important decision for the camp cook to make is which ones of the many to choose. Some of the menus in this pamphlet are specific in their recommendations. Here are some notes about lightweight foods for your pack.

## Fruits

Except for dried apples, most dried fruits contain moisture that hasn't been driven out completely in the drying process. This fact makes them ideal for a flavorful snack on the trail or as a quick dessert. At the same time, their moisture content *will* allow them to spoil from mold more quickly than a food completely dehydrated and wrapped in a container of some kind.

You're lucky to be able to choose from dates, figs, and such "exotic" fruits as freeze-dried strawberries and blueberries, as well as the more common dried foods we have mentioned. You'll appreciate other qualities in dried foods, too. Aside from savings in space and weight (up to 80 percent in many foods), you'll find a fascinating variety in flavor, texture, and color. Many new foods needing no refrigeration are found on grocers' shelves.

## Dry Grains

Plant seeds that dry upon ripening are longtime favorites in camp or on the trail. A few of the most popular are oats, beans, rice, peas, nuts, wheat, barley, and lentils.

Whole-grain barley and wheat, remember, are delicious to eat out-of-hand. And wheat eaten this way provides a long-lasting and flavorful chew.

## Dried Foods

Dried or dehydrated foods these days are worthwhile achievements of the food technologists. Removal of moisture alone is no great trick, but preservation of flavor, color, and texture while it's being done is a tough job. As you use dehydrated foods, you'll see that the job has been done well. Charge your menus with variety by simple moistening of these foods. Follow directions carefully, using the correct amount of water — just enough to mix the flakes or powders of these dehydrated specials — and you will enjoy them. Try these:

• Dehydrated baked beans
• Dehydrated vegetables
• Minute rice
• Powdered eggs
• Dehydrated soups
• Onion flakes
• Dried tomato sauce or paste
• Dehydrated potatoes of a number of types
• Powdered skim milk
• Prepared cocoa or chocolate milk powders

Remember that dehydrated soups make delicious combinations with other foods.

Bread and Biscuits

The prepared mix and corner bakery are fine and convenient additions to our modern life. But the bannock, biscuit, or raised bread that is made in your own special way is an unbeatable satisfier of appetites.

Don't forget, either, that ground, whole-wheat grains carry a greater share of nutrition than any bleached flour possibly can—even "enriched" kinds.

Everybody knows that a "sourdough" means a hardy prospector. But perhaps he was also a man who liked bread but didn't have the chance to get to the corner bakery very often. You can be a skilled baker of sourdough biscuits, and here's how to make your starter.

Sourdough is basically a culture of yeast in flour and water. Every time you use it for bread or biscuits, save about a cupful of the starter, adding more flour and water so that the yeasts will ferment some more for the next time you need it. (Pancakes with sourdough are delicious, too.)

Dissolve a packet of dry yeast in a cup of water, milk, sour milk, or buttermilk. Add 1 cup or more of flour, making a smooth batter. A spoonful of sugar will speed fermentation of the yeast buds, but it's not absolutely necessary to the recipe.

Let your starter stand overnight near the stove or fire—or in the sun—until it seems to grow and is full of bubbles.

Use an earthenware jar or glass container, because the acids in sourdough can eventually eat a hole right through metal. Guaranteed not to mistreat your digestive tract, though!

You can mix dough right in your flour bag —pour water right into a pit made in the mix and stir it with a "twixer" stick until a ball of dough forms around the stick. When the ball revolves in opposite direction, remove it.

**DAMPER or ASH BREAD.** How primitive can you get? Pat dough into an inch-thick cake and put it on several sweet green leaves. Sweep coals and ash to one side and lay cake and leaves on hot hearth. Cover with leaves, then with gray ashes and hot coals. Test in 10 minutes by pushing dry stem of grass into it — if it comes out clean your bread is done.

**TWIST.** Peel a club of "sweet wood," wood with a neutral taste, 2 inches thick and 2 feet long—point ends. Preheat club near fire. Make dough. Wet the hot club and then roll a long "sausage" of dough and twist it around the club. Stick end of club in ground so dough bakes over fire. Keep turning as it browns—reverse ends of club to even out browning. You can keep an eye on this bread, so don't let it bake to quickly or burn.

**BANNOCK.** Canoe-country standby is this frying-pan loaf. Recipes vary, but the biscuit dough works fine. Make an inch-thick loaf as big as your pan. Don't grease the pan. Bake for 7 or 8 minutes over slow coals to brown the bottom, then tilt pan almost upright before a brighter fire to finish off the top. Test with stem in another 7 or 8 minutes. No hurry — it'll wait.

# Dutch Oven Cooking

Here's a well-rounded utensil that's best to use at your base (or permanent) camp—or when you have several buddies or a faithful pack animal to help in carrying extra weight. Made of thick cast aluminum or cast iron, the Dutch oven has a recessed or flanged cover that allows you to place hot coals on top while you rest the oven itself on hot coals from your fire. Heat can be adjusted by wise choice of the quantity of the coals used, and it's quite easy to check on the cooking progress by inspecting the oven's contents. Never place your oven over flames but on coals removed from fire. Bake almost anything in the Dutch oven that you'd bake in the oven at home. That includes pies, cakes, breads, biscuits, and bannock. Stews, casseroles, chicken, steaks, and roasts respond equally well to the Dutch oven treatment. To clean your oven, preheat it, rub with butter, and wipe with paper towel.

**BISCUITS.** Use mix or biscuit recipe. Preheat oven. Turn dough out on lightly floured board and kneed 30 seconds. Roll to ½-inch thickness. Cut squares with knife or remove ends from small can to cut round biscuits. Flour edge of can. Press, don't twist. Don't roll or reknead dough scraps; press them together gently to make a biscuit-sized piece. Handled dough or biscuits get "sad." Put cut floured biscuits in bottom of ungreased oven with some space between. Put lid on and set oven on coals; add coals to lid—it must be quite hot. Check in 10 minutes; test with straw. They may take 12 or 15 minutes to complete baking.

**PHILMONT RANGER COBBLER.** Here is an easy method of making a fruit cobbler in a Dutch oven. It serves six to eight.

YOU WILL NEED:

2 No. 2½ cans of fruit, such as cherries, peaches, fruit cocktail, etc.
1 small box of biscuit mix
1 tsp. cinnamon
¼ cup sugar
¼ stick of butter

Preheat oven and lid by placing on edge near fire. Pull good supply of coals out to side of fire and place oven over coals. Dump in two cans of fruit, liquid and all. If fresh fruit is used, add water and sugar to keep moist. Replace oven lid and bring fruit to a boil—no coals are needed on lid at this time. Open box of biscuit mix, make cup in powder, add water, and with "twixer stick" make small dumpling-sized balls of biscuit mix (about 1 to 1½ inches in diameter). Drop these into boiling fruit to cover top of fruit. Let bottom coals go out but add liberal supply of coals to top of oven. Replace the coals often to ensure good heat. You cannot burn this cobbler by adding too much heat on lid. Add butter to top of dough, sprinkle with cinnamon and sugar mixture, and replace top of oven.

**POT ROAST.** Dredge a 4-pound roast and brown all sides in hot fat in oven. Add ½ inch of water, put on lid; add coals to lid. Simmer 2 to 3 hours, adding water as needed, until tender; add peeled potato, onion, and carrot per diner for the last 45 minutes.

**BAKED POTATO.** Scrub well one big potato per person. Prick skin with a fork and grease lightly. Wrap tightly in foil and put on plate set on pebbles in hot oven. Cover, add coals to lid, bake for an hour or so. Test with splinter — meaty crumbs sticking to wood show potato is done. Slash an X in foil and potato and pinch to push it open. Add butter and salt.

**OVEN-FRIED CHICKEN.** Use ½ fryer per person; cut into pieces. Dip in cold water, wipe dry; shake in seasoned flour in paper bag. Put 2 tablespoons of fat or cooking oil in hot oven and brown chicken pieces all over. Then turn skin-side down, cover with lid; add coals. Bake, basting occasionally, for 15 minutes. Turn pieces over and cook until tender, about 25 minutes.

**BAKED APPLE.** Wash, core large apple per serving. Fill hole with sugar, raisins, and dab of butter — cinnamon, if desired. Put apples on greased plate and add some water. Put plate in hot oven on three pebbles to prevent burning. Cover and bake for about 30 minutes.

# Aluminum Foil Cooking

There are probably still some old-time traditionalists of the outdoors who won't admit that aluminum foil is fit for anything but wrapping—or who say that this material is used only by city folks and sissies experimenting around the backyard barbecue. Without trying to argue against tradition, let's look at some of the things that well-planned use of foil can do for us. One author has written without apology to any old-timer, ". . . the use of aluminum foil in outdoor (and indoor) cooking is a major factor in the culinary arts. Aluminum foil can cook many kinds of foods in many ways in a manner far superior to any other method."*

*J. D. Bates, Jr., in *The Outdoor Cook's Bible*.

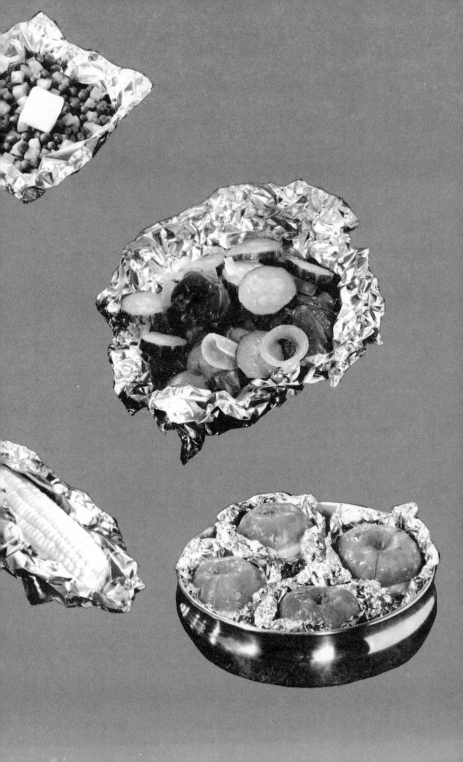

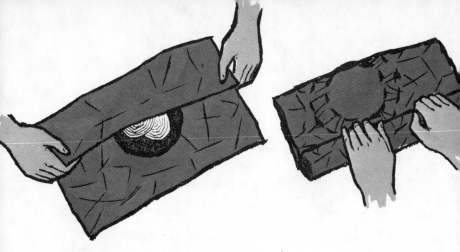

Here is how to wrap food in aluminum foil for cooking.

Add these plus factors: light-weight, durability, low cost, saves carrying heavier cooking utensils. These are all to the good.

How do you choose among all the weights and finishes of foil you can buy at the grocery? How do you use the stuff efficiently? These tips should help.

The heavy-duty foil is usually the best as a cooking wrapper. If only lightweight foil is available, use double thicknesses to avoid the problem of punch-through, ripping, or tearing.

It's important—to the way your food is cooked and to your peace of mind—that foil cooking packages be sealed tightly. This will retain steam and juices. At the same time, a secure wrap will keep ashes and dirt out of the meal. (Salt, pepper, and an herb or two are sufficient decoration and flavoring.)

There is no formula that you can follow exactly in telling when your foil-wrapped food is cooked to the king's taste. The knowledge comes mostly after you experiment and practice—along with pretty consistent practice in building the same sort of cooking fire each time you have responsibility as chief cook.

**FISH FRY.** Double a 2-foot-long piece of foil. Rub it with bacon fat or margarine. Wipe the fish after cleaning it. Place it on the greased foil and wrap it, crimping the ends of the foil packet. Place packet on glowing coals. After 5 minutes, turn packet over, cook 5 minutes more. Open and salt fish.

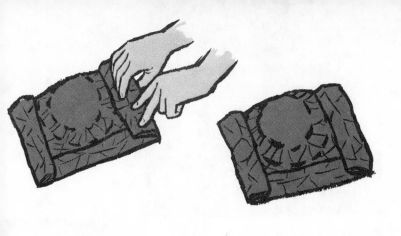

**BURGER IN ARMOR.** Wash, peel, and cut in ⅓-inch slices a medium potato and a large carrot. Double a piece of foil into an 18-inch square and spread the vegetables on one-quarter of it, leaving a 2-inch margin around them. Pat ¼-pound hamburger into a ¾-inch cake and put it beside the vegetables. Salt the vegetables but not the meat; pepper if you like. Add slices of onion and a dab of butter. Fold empty side of the foil over until edges are even. Turn a ½-inch fold over and crease; fold twice more, pressing flat. Do the same at both ends to seal packet. There is (or should be) room for expansion. Set on tempered coals and cover with more. Cook 15 or 20 minutes. Eat burger directly from foil.

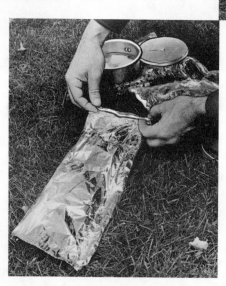

## BISCUITS or SHORTCAKE.

Use mix or favorite recipe and make dough adding 1 tablespoon of sugar per cup of dry ingredients for shortcake. Mix with water right in the carrying bag, stirring with stick until dough makes ball on stick. Flour hands, pat dough into 1/2-inch thick biscuit with minimum handling. Grease a 12-inch square of doubled foil, and fold as for burger recipe. Bake in coals 10 minutes, turning packet to even browning. Leave plenty of room in packet for dough to rise. Eat as is or save to combine with fruit.

# Cooking Chicken

Chickens are in plentiful supply, inexpensive and make an excellent meal that is easy to cook outdoors. Barbecued over an open fire, they are delicious.

Primitive way is to spit chicken on a peeled stick run from vent to neck. Truss bird securely so it will turn with spit. If wings or legs stick out, they'll burn before bird is done. Test doneness by twisting leg; when thigh is loose, the entire bird should be OK.

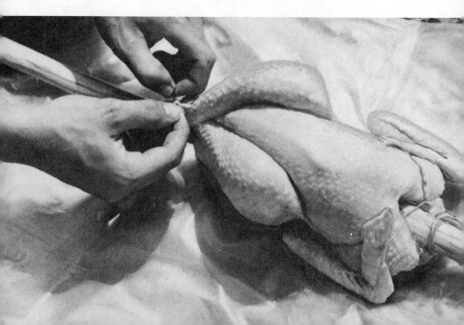

Another way to do it is to suspend the bird from a dingle stick to one side of the fire over a foil or other drip pan. Prepare bird as usual and truss the legs and wings. Then run skewers through wings and upper body. Be sure the drumsticks are snugged down and that the wing tips don't stick out. Now hang the bird from the dingle stick by running a thong under the skewer. While cooking, turn it now and then so both back and front get the heat, and when about half done, swap skewers so top and bottom are done equally. Baste the breast particularly, as it tends to dry out before the rest cooks.

# Cooking Fish

**PAN-FRIED.** Heat ⅛ inch of margarine, bu[tter] cooking oil, or bacon fat in the frying [pan.] Coat the fish with seasoned flour and fry [to] golden brown, rocking pan now and the[n to] prevent sticking.

Any good cook hates waste. A thrifty Scout is no exception.

Any fish can be wasted if it doesn't reach your cooking utensil in the best possible condition. There are three things you must do to keep that "condition."

• Clean fish soon after they're caught.

• Keep them cool.

• Keep them dry, but keep them away from sun and breezes.

Clean fish by slitting them with a sharp knife from the vent to the gills. Pull out the entrails, remove all of the gills and any dark matter that you find under the membrane beneath the backbone. An old (but clean) toothbrush is a good tool for this.

Then wipe the fish dry—inside and out. Use as little water as possible. Remove scales from the outside when necessary. If the fish is a trout, the head is sometimes left on.

### Sizzle, Steam, or Dry Heat?

Whatever cooking method you use for fish, remember that overcooking and excessive heat are destroyers of good fish. (The only exception to this is the high temperatures needed in the first stages of baking or planking such oily fish as mackerel.)

A fish fry is delicious when it's properly done. The process is quick and the results are tempting. Bread, cracker crumbs, flour, or cornmeal are good coatings to use for frying; use deep fat. When one side turns golden brown, a thick cut of fish is ready to turn. Thinner cuts are probably already done.

The other ways of cooking fish are almost as simple. You can find many recipes with instructions for boiling, baking, broiling, stuffing, or marinating. You'll want to try stuffing or serving with sauces, too.

**POACHED.** For the delicacy blue trout, you must have fr[e]
caught fish. Do not wipe off slime—this is what turns bl[ue]
handle as little as possible. Add 1/4 cup of vinegar to
enough water to cover fish. Slip fish one at a time into bo[iling]
water, so boiling won't stop. Poach 6 minutes.

**FOILED.** Take 2 feet of foil and double it. Rub margarine
or bacon fat on the foil and roll fish singly, crimpling ends of
foil packet. Place packet on glowing coals. After 5 minutes,
turn packet over, cook 5 minutes more. Open and salt fish.
Simple and neat.

**SMOKED.** Chop up red cedar twigs and put 2 inches deep in large pot. Behead and clean fish. String fish by tails on sticks and hang from pot rim. Cover pot and put it over fire. Fish should be done in about an hour — the flesh tender and juicy, the skin tough.

**STEAMED.** Simplest way to cook trout. Cut a stick for each fish, 4 inches or so longer than fish. Point one end. Tie trout to stick at tail and gills, head toward the point. Push stick into shallow coals until heads are partly covered. Steam for about 10 minutes.

# Selecting and Cooking Meat

Entire books have been written about how to work cooking magic with meats from large wild animals, rabbits, and wild game birds. But because not many Scouts will live off the land during their hikes and camping trips, we'll leave you to read far more information on this specialty in books by experts.

The menus and recipes in this pamphlet are designed to help you plan and cook using foods that are easy to find in your local markets and stores.

## Keep It Fresh

If you're going to be several hours on the way to your first campsite of the trip and if weather conditions may cause spoilage of your fresh meat, start with meat that's right from the freezer. Well wrapped in waterproof foil or plastic and insulated with a few layers of newspaper, fresh meats will stay in good shape for several hours, sometimes as long as a day.

## Grill, Pan, or Pot?

Good meats are to be treated with care in their cooking. And the way that most beginning cooks ruin most meats most of the time is to cook them for so long that the finished product has lost flavor, texture, and most of its juice!

With a frying pan or griddle as the cooking surface, meats can be seared on either side just long enough to seal in the juices, then moved to a part of the fire that's not the hottest for the rest of their cooking.

When you're broiling meat such as steak, searing can be done in a few short seconds on either side by placing the meat directly on the coals.

## Selecting Meat

If you're lucky enough to find a store where the butcher is behind the counter instead of hidden behind a group of mirrors, the man with knife and cleaver will be a helpful friend when it comes to picking good meat for your outdoor cooking. He'll even point out the characteristics of a good cut of beef or tell you how to judge lamp or veal by its appearance. Then you can buy a piece of meat with the assurance that it's tender and full of the flavor that a careful and thrifty buyer deserves.

On the other hand, even with prewrapping and "convenience packaging," it is still possible to pick a steak or roast that will do you proud when you yell, "Come and get it!" Here are some things to look for.

*Beef.*—Steaks and roasts should be "marbled" with small flecks of white fat throughout the lean. Color should be a bright red when meat is sliced—though exposure to air will darken the surface relatively quickly. Most beef from grass-fed or corn-fed beef has white fat. Some good beef has a stronger yellow coloring to its fat—a result of the beef animal's diet. If the other signs

of quality are present (bright red color, flecks of fat in lean tissue) don't be afraid.

*Pork.* — Color of lean meat (whether roasts, chops, or other cuts) in fresh pork is a medium pink with a touch of gray. Fat is white and firm. Fresh hams, shoulders, or other roasts should have most of the fat trimmed from the outside to speed cooking. *Caution:* Always be sure that pork is completely cooked — no pink should show under your carving knife.

*Veal.* — Small amounts of fat are a characteristic of veal, and the lean is not so firm as beef. Color is a sort of gray-pink. A deeper red tone indicates that the animal from which the meat was carved was probably older and going toward the "baby beef" classification.

*Lamb.*—You'll want cuts that show a touch of fat here and there in the lean portions. As spring lamb ages toward the status of "muttonhood," the meat's color becomes a darker red. The flavor becomes somewhat stronger, too. Lamb is especially good after marination, or with a touch of garlic clove rubbed over the meat's surface before cooking. You'll note that a sprig of fresh or dried mint is a good touch with lamb, too.

*Smoked, Corned, or Sausage Meats.*—Here, you depend pretty

**KABOB or SHISH KEBAB.** Use a metal skewer or a 2-foot straight stick (from unwanted growth) about as thick as a lead pencil and point one end. Better peel it. Cut tender beefsteak or lamb shoulder into 1-inch squares; it may be marinated if need be. Peel onions and cut lengthwise once; separate the layers. To get fancy, cut up bacon, quarter tomatoes, slice cucumbers, or quarter green peppers, as you wish, too. Alternate slices of meat with vegetables on skewer, then put over or beside hot coals, turning to broil evenly. Let everyone do his own. Eat from stick.

much on the brand name, and on your own preference. Each meat packer (and there are some very good regional and local firms in the field) has its own recipes. Ask the cook in your house for the names of those meats you've eaten and liked many times at the home table. The same rule applies whether you want to carry along a whole lamb, a tin of corned beef, or some slices of luncheon meat.

No matter what kind of meat you decide to buy, you'll find a wide range of prices among the cuts available. You may wonder which are the best for such outdoor dishes as stew, shish kebab, or various kinds of steaks. We

could give you a long list of choices, but recommend that Mom's advice in this department is valuable. The man who sells quality meats is often glad to help you with information from his experience and knowledge.

# One-Pot Meal

The one-pot meal goes by many names. You might call it stew, casserole, chowder, gumbo, or slum gullion.

Name it what you will, the meal-in-one dish is the outdoor cook's best ally in his race against the clamour of a number of hungry men whose digestive tracts have begun to grumble.

Convenient? Sure, it's that. What's more, the meal in a single dish is a real challenge to the cook who yearns to invent a taste during his duty as chef for the hour. Perhaps the top advantage in this type of cooking is . . . really good eating!

**ONE-POT MEAL.** Beef, veal, lamb, pork, chicken, or fish can be used. If you use a red meat, dredge it first in flour and sear it in hot fat before putting it into the pot. Select vegetables that go with the meat or fish you are using, but use raw ones so that they can be cooked for a long time without becoming overdone. Add 1½ cups of hot water. Cover the pot tightly. It will cook in a bean hole that has been previously prepared. (Dig a hole 1½ feet wider and a foot deeper than your pot. Line it with dry, flat, nonexplosive stones. On a stick bridge lay a big crisscross fire. Keep feeding it until the hole is full of embers and the stones white hot.) Scoop the embers out of the hole and lower the pot into it. Surround and cover the bucket with embers. Then put on a layer of dirt. Be sure to leave the bail handle of the pot sticking out so you can locate it later. After the meal has cooked the time required carefully excavate your pot. Use particular caution to make certain that the cover does not open and let dirt in.

## SLUM GULLION

MENU-Slum Gullion—a one-pot meal for patrol of six Scouts.

Bread      Hot and/or cold drink

Jam        Fruit for dessert

## QUANTITIES

2½ lbs. hamburger (packaged and frozen in advance)

6-8 medium potatoes

1/3 lb. bacon

3 medium onions

2 8-oz. cans tomato sauce or tomato puree

2/3 lb. cheddar cheese

12 oz. cookies

1½ loaves bread

1 1-lb. jar jam

¼ lb. butter

salt and pepper

1 jar instant coffee, cocoa, or ½ qt. milk per person

1 No. 2½ can prune plums or fruit cocktail

## PREPARATION

1. Place pot of water to be used for hot drinks, dishwater, etc., over fire.

2. Put 2-3 cups of water and 1 tsp. salt in cooking pot. Place over fire.

3. Peel, quarter, and wash potatoes; add to water and bring to boil.

While Potatoes Are Cooking —

• Dice bacon in ½-inch squares and fry crisp brown in the bottom of another pot.

• Add finely chopped onion when bacon is about fried out.

• Add crumbled hamburger, a little at a time, and stir off bottom of pan while cooking.

• Add tomato puree.

• Cut cheese into ½-inch cubes and add to hamburger mixture; place over a low fire and stir frequently until cheese is melted.

• Drain potatoes and add to hamburger mixture. If pots are small or you have an enlarged food issue because of a larger patrol, you may want to mix the slum gullion by using both pots.

• Serve slum gullion on bread. Open jam and fruit and prepare hot drinks or milk.

*Before Sitting Down to Supper— After Water Has Been Removed for Hot Drinks Be Sure To Fill Up the Hot Water Pot and Place Over Fire To Boil for Dishwater.*

# POLICY ON LIQUID FUELS

In Scout camping, it is recommended that natural wood or charcoal be used for cooking, and that flashlights or electric battery lamps be used for lighting. This applies especially to troop camping and camporees.

The need for adapting to special conditions such as the lack of natural wood for fuel or cooking on campway tours would only be occasional and never routine.

When gasoline is used for cooking and lighting, it is the fuel which is dangerous, not the stoves and lanterns. For safety reasons, Scouts should not be involved in the storage of gasoline, the handling of it in the filling of stoves and lanterns, or the lighting of it.

Council health and safety committee may permit by local action the use of gasoline in the following way: On those limited occasions when gasoline stoves and lanterns are used, they are to be restricted to adults only. The only exception to this rule should be on those tours and high-adventure trail trips where no other fuel is available or practical except gasoline. When that situation occurs, older Scouts and Explorers may be permitted with proper training to use gasoline-fueled equipment under adult supervision. Adherence to high safety standards must be required when this practice is permitted.

Under certain conditions when an artificial fuel is needed, LP gas* is convenient for cooking and lighting. An example of this situation would be when camping on a trip in a park where wood and charcoal fires are not permitted. Here again, proper safety control, training, and adult supervision are required.

Empty LP cylinders for portable stoves and lanterns may explode in a fire and, therefore, must never be put in with burnable trash.

In accordance with the long-standing rule of *no flames in tents,* liquid fuel stoves and lanterns should never be used in tents.

The use of liquid fuels for starting any type of fire is prohibited. This includes damp wood, charcoal, and ceremonial campfires. Solid type starters are just as effective and much safer.

All types of heaters, including those which use liquid fuels, consume oxygen and must only be used in well ventilated areas. When used in tents, cabins, camper-trucks, and trailers, there is not only a fire danger but also lives can be lost from asphyxiation. Deaths from carbon-monoxide poisoning have been reported when charcoal burners were used in an enclosed area.

*LP gas means liquefied gas (compressed propane or butane).

# Books About Cooking

**PREPARED BY THE AMERICAN
LIBRARY ASSOCIATION/BOY
SCOUT ADVISORY COMMITTEE**

## Scout Literature

*Camping* merit badge pamphlet and *Fieldbook*.

## Other Books

Barker, Harriett, *Supermarket Backpacker*. Greatlakes Living Press, 1977.

*Better Homes and Gardens New Cook Book*, rev. ed., Meredith Corp., 1976.

Blanchard, Marjorie Page, *The Outdoor Cookbook*. Franklin Watts, 1977.

Cross, Margaret and Fiske, Jean, *Backpacker's Cookbook*. Ten Speed Press, 1974.

Getzoff, Carole, *The Natural Cook's First Book*. Dodd, Mead & Co., 1973.

Holm, Don, *Old-Fashioned Dutch Oven Cookbook*. Caxton, 1969

Paul, Aileen, *Kids Camping*. Doubleday, 1973.

Schwartz, Paula Dunaway, *You Can Cook*. Atheneum, 1976.

Thomas, Dian, *Roughing It Easy: A Unique Ideabook for Camping and Cooking*. Brigham Young University Press, 1974.

Thomas, Dian, *Roughing It Easy, Two*. Warner Books, 1978.

Zarchy, Harry, *Let's Go Camping*. Alfred A. Knopf, 1951.

## Pamphlets

"Family. fare; a guide to good nutrition," rev., 1978. Single copy free from Office of Governmental and Public Affairs, U.S. Department of Agriculture, Washington, DC 20250.

## Magazines

*Camping Journal*
*Backpacker*